Real Estate Investing

How to Invest in Real Estate with Little Money and No Experience

By Mark Bresett

Table of Contents

Introduction

Congratulations on purchasing your personal copy of Real Estate Investing: How to Invest in Real Estate with Little Money and No Experience. Thank you for doing so.

The following chapters will discuss some of the many methods and strategies that you can use in order to get started in the real estate market without having a lot of money or experience in the field. Real estate can be a really profitable investment opportunity, but with all of the options that are out there and the higher risk with some of your choices, it can be hard to know how to get started. But when you are ready to get into the market and learn about all the possibilities, this is the guidebook that will help you out.

In this guidebook, we are going to spend some time talking about the different topics that you need to know about the real estate market. We will talk about the different investment opportunities that are available in the market, the market cycle and the best times to make your purchases and sell, some of the strategies used for making money in real estate, how to protect your assets, common mistakes that you should avoid as a beginner and so much more. When you are done, you will be ready to take on your investment of choice and really make a high profit in no time!

There are plenty of books on this subject on the market, thanks again for choosing this one! Every effort was made to ensure it is full of as much useful information as possible. Please enjoy!

Congratulations on purchasing your personal copy of the name of the book. Thank you for doing so.

Chapter 1

Types of Investments Available in Real Estate

There are several options that you can choose when you are ready to join the world of real estate investing. These options offer their own unique challenges and risks, but they can make it more interesting when it comes to putting your money to work. The option that you choose often depends on the market in your area, how much you are able to spend, and what interests you the most. The top options for real estate investing include:

Residential real estate

Residential real estate is great any time that you want to work with individuals and families and make an income from the rent they pay each month. These would include various properties including vacation houses, townhouses, apartments, and houses. There are benefits of each one. Homes are popular because these usually go to families who are willing to stick around for the long term, making a steady stream of income. But apartments are going to generate more income because they can house more people, but the longevity of the tenants often goes down.

Commercial real estate

This investment opportunity is going to include things like office buildings. With this option, you would get funding in order to construct a building that has individual offices that you can lease out to business owners and companies. While these companies are inside your building, they are going to pay you rent to keep using the property. Often these investments are going to include leases that last for at least several years, allowing the company to be secure and not have to move around a lot, and it provides you the opportunity to get a steady stream of income for the long term.

Industrial real estate

Industrial real estate is another investment that you can make. This one will include things like car washes, storage units, and distribution centers as well as other real estate that is special-purpose and will generate income from customers who are using the facility temporarily. These may have a big upfront cost to the investor, but they will often have a good service revenue stream and fees (such as the coin-operated cleaners at the car wash), which can help to increase your revenue in no time.

Retail real estate

These investments consist of things like retail storefronts, strip malls, and shopping malls. There are many different businesses that would be willing to pay rent, especially if the retail space is near high traffic areas. Sometimes the lease will just include a monthly payment from the tenants, and other times you may also receive a percentage of the sales from each tenant that is inside your space; this can produce a high level of income if the businesses are really popular a

These are expensive to start, but with the right retail space, you can get more than one business into the same area, allowing you to get rental income from more than one place at the same time. You can choose the size of the retail space that you want to go with and while a bigger space is going to cost more to purchase or to make, if you are able to fill it up with more tenants and it is in a location that high traffic, you will quickly get your investment back.

Mixed-use real estate

Mixed-use real estate is a good option when you would like to combine some of the categories above into just one project. You will need to have significant assets to make this happen, but it can help to bring about a good return on investment when people start to rent out the building that you have available.

A good example of this is when an investor makes an investment to build a mixed office building that is three stories high and is surrounded by some retail shops. The investor would be able to rent out each of the floors in the office building, bringing in quite a bit of income each month. Then since there is a shopping and retail center around the office building, it is possible to rent out those buildings as well to thinks like a clothing store, a gym, and some restaurants. There is a lot of potential of who would like to rent these areas so it is likely that you can fill them up quickly and with long-term tenants. You must have a good amount to invest to start with, since these are expensive, but you will quickly get the money back, and more.

Flipping homes

If you are not interested in keeping hold of the property and renting it out to individuals or companies, you may want to consider flipping homes as your investing type. With this option, you will find a good property that is in a decent neighborhood, but for some little reason is being sold way under value. You can get in on the good price, make some changes and updates, and then sell it back up at the level that other similar homes in the area are going for.

Flipping homes can be tricky. While you own the home, you are responsible for making the monthly payments, dealing with insurance, and other payments that come with maintaining the house. You need to make sure that you are actually getting a good deal on the home and that the market is doing well enough that you can sell it again soon. Making the changes quickly and getting the home back on the market can help you to reduce your costs and increase your profits. But if you do the process properly, flipping homes can give you a great return on investment.

Real estate investing is a great opportunity because it offers so many options for you to choose with. Based on your personal preferences when it comes to investing and how much risk you would like to take, there are different options that can help you to get the return on investment that you want. Before getting into the market, consider some of these real estate investment types so that you can come up with the winning strategy.

Chapter 2
Understanding the Market Conditions
in Your Area

Before you make a purchase in real estate and try to use it to make some money, it is important to understand what is going on in the market before you make a purchase. If the housing market is down and you aren't seeing much in terms of sales of homes, this may not be a good time to try flipping a home. You may be stuck with the home for some time. If you are able to afford the payment for a bit you can get the home for a really affordable price in these market conditions and earn more later, but you could be holding onto a house for a long time. But, when market conditions for selling homes are low, the need for rentals is higher and you may also be able to get an inexpensive home and rent it out for a good profit.

As you can see, the market conditions surrounding the real estate industry are going to greatly influence what you are able to do when making purchases and either renting out or selling a home. Each market goes through an ebb and flow between the various conditions, but it also goes through a cycle. This helps to make it easier to determine when is the right time to get into this market and when it may be time to withdraw and wait it out a bit.

In order to determine the right time to get into the market, you need to understand the market cycle. Remember that you can be considering this type of investment at any point of the cycle and that this ends up going round and round. Some of the aspects found in the real estate market cycle include:

- The peak: this is when the prices are at their all-time high. At the same time, inventory is down so there is usually a lot of competition to get the homes that are available and usually there are several offers for each property, many above the asking price. This is not the best time to enter the market because you will end up paying more than the property is worth and could get into a bidding war. On the other hand, this is a great time to sell your home because many people are looking and there aren't many options.

- The tipping point: at this point, the prices of homes have gotten too high and they are going to start falling, which allows it to compensate for the high prices and the overbuilding that occurred earlier on. Foreclosure rates start to go up and many homeowners are going to have trouble paying their mortgage. They still won't be able to sell because they owe more than the home is worth and no one will make a purchase.

- The decline: in this part of the cycle, the prices are going to continue to fall and there are going to be a lot of foreclosures on the market. People are pretty fearful of purchasing at this point because they are scared of getting into something they can't afford later, which causes an issue with a lot of inventory on the market, driving prices down even more.

- The bottom: here is where the prices of the homes will kind of even out and get as low as they will during the process. This is a good place to make some purchases because you can get some great homes at a good process. Many investors will choose to make their purchases out of all the inventory that is available. Deals are all around and making a cash flow is going to be high.

- The climb: over time, buyers are going to gain some more confidence in purchasing homes and they will start going out there to make the purchases. This is going to lead to more sales in the real estate industry, less inventory, and the prices will start to go up.

As you can see, this cycle can keep repeating over and over again and figuring out the perfect time to get into the market will help you to make as much money as possible in this game. The length of the cycle is gong to vary based on the area you are in and you will find that the decline and the bottom are often going to last longer than the climb and the peak because it does take a while for the buyers to come back and make purchases.

Now, before you get into the market, it is important to figure out where in the market your current area is. If you notice that your area is at the tipping point, this is probably not a good place to make a purchase because prices are high and interested buyers are low. You won't make much of a profit off these properties. But if you notice that your area is at the bottom and there seems to be more confidence in the real estate market, you may want to make a purchase while the prices are low and deals are good. The hope here is that by the time you make some of the adjustments to the house and finish with closing, the market will be into more of a climb or in the peak, and you can profit even more from that.

The best way to get familiar with the market is to gain experience. In the beginning, you may have some trouble recognizing the signs between each part of the cycle, but over time you are going to get better at this and can make purchases at the right time. There isn't necessarily a big shift between each of the parts, but if you notice that home prices keep going up like crazy every year or so, after a few years you may be ready for a tipping point to occur.

Learning about the market conditions is one of the best ways to determine if it is the right time to get into the real estate market and can help to increase your profits. You can spend time watching what is going on in the market in order to get the best deals on your properties before selling or renting out when the market is higher and you can make the biggest profit.

Chapter 3
Different Strategies to Successfully Find Properties

Now that you are ready to get into the real estate market, it is a good idea to find what strategy you want to use to make some money on your investment. There are a couple strategies that you can use and you should think them through before deciding on the property that you want to purchase. For example, if you want to use a property as a rental home, you would pick things out differently compared to picking out a home that you want to flip quickly. Here are some of the different strategies that you may consider when getting started with real estate investing.

Buy and hold

The first strategy for real estate investing is one of the most common as well. The buy and hold method is going to involve purchasing a property for a good price and then renting it out for a long period of time. This is one of the easiest forms of investing that you can choose. Basically, you are going to get your money back from renting out this property to someone else who would like to live there, and you will receive this income monthly as they pay it to you. This is a great cash flow option that will allow you to keep renting out the building for many years, or just a few while you get out of the bottom of the market cycle and are able to sell the property at a much higher price.

There are many advantages that come with choosing this form of investing. One of these advantages is that not only are you making a little bit of income through the rent, you can also use some of it to pay the mortgage down each month, while not having to use your own personal money. This makes it easier to decrease the balance of your principal on the property and will increase the equity on the property. You can use this equity to get more properties later on or it can increase your profits when you do sell the property.

To get started with the principle of buy and hold, you need to learn how to evaluate the opportunities and deals that are in your area. One big mistake that new investors will make with this particular strategy is that they make bad deals simply because they don't really understand how property evaluation works. In addition, new investors will fail with this option because they don't properly estimate their expenses to run the property, they pick out bad tenants to live in the property, and they don't do the right steps to manage the property. These are mistakes that you can avoid with a bit of knowledge and a good strategy, but many new investors lose out on a lot of money because of poor decisions with the buy and hold strategy.

In order to successfully use this strategy, you as the investor will need to learn how to identify the ebbs and flows of your market cycle (which we discussed in the chapter above). When you notice that the properties they are interested in are at what is considered a low point (meaning that the prices are low but the inventory is high), they will make the purchase of their chosen property. Then when the market goes back uphill and it starts to get over-heated, an investor who is using buy and hold will stop making purchases of properties because these are going to be too expensive for them to handle and still make a profit. They will wait until the market settles back down. During some of these slow times, the investor may hold on to their properties or they can sell them to make some more money.

There are several methods that you can use with this. Some investors choose to purchase the property with the intention of selling it in the long run. But since they purchased it during a low point in the market cycle, they may have some time to wait before they are able to make a good profit on the property. During this time, which could be a few years, the investor will rent out the property, making a little bit of income and paying down what they owe on the mortgage as well. Then when the market goes back up and the tenant is gone, they will flip the house and sell it, making a big profit compared to if they sold the property right away.

Some buy and hold investors choose to never sell their properties, though. They will continue to rent out the property and make the rental income while still making a little bit of income on the side. They will keep going until the mortgage is paid off and then all the income, minus the taxes and insurance, can go straight to them. If they decide to sell after this, you may find that they use Seller Financing for this to attract more buyers.

Those who are using buy and hold can own more than one property at a time, increasing the amount that they make each month by combining the income together. As a beginner, you will probably want to just start with one property and start paying it down a bit and making some income before moving over to two or more, but this is a great way to turn your investment into a full-time income.

Flipping Homes

Another option that you can use as your strategy in real estate is house flipping. This is the one that you will see on many popular television shows, but they often make it seem more glamorous and profitable than it is in real life. But if you are good at finding some deals on homes in your area, you can turn your investment into a good profit by flipping houses.

The idea behind this strategy is that you find a good piece of real estate that has lots of great features, but it has something that is wrong with it that is driving the price down and giving you a good deal. You can snatch this home up for that price and then make a few improvements before selling it to make a profit. If you do this right, the home can sell for a price comparable to other homes in that area, while still providing you with a good profit.

Most investors who go into flipping homes will focus on a single family home since these are the easiest to use with this option. A good rule of thumb that you can use for flipping homes is the 70% rule. With this one, you will only purchase homes that are being sold for 70% of their current value, less any of the costs of rehab. For example, let's say that a home is worth $100,000 in its current area if it were sold in good condition, but you are going to have to put about $20,000 into it to make it look nice. According to the rule of 70%, you would not purchase this home for more than $50,000 to make a good profit. You could then make the adjustments to the home and then sell it for that $100,000 when you are done. Remember that this is just something to consider and picking out the home that you will use, while also considering the costs, will vary depending on each unique situation.

If you want to make money with flipping homes, you need to be fast. The longer you hold onto the home after you make the purchase, the more money you will spend on the mortgage, taxes, and insurance in addition to your closing costs and the costs to fix it up. You also need to keep in mind that most homes sit on the market for a few months at least and that you will still have a bit of time for closing to be complete. Make sure to put some of these numbers into your calculations, and make sure that you are able to cover your current costs along with the cost of the home while you own it before you make a purchase.

There is a lot of work that goes into flipping homes and you will need to be active in the work the whole way to ensure it is done well and as quickly as possible. But if you find a good deal in the home that you choose and you can make a sale that you are happy with, it is easy to make a great profit and a great return on investment with this strategy.

Wholesaling

Wholesaling is another option that you can go with when looking for a way to make some money in real estate. With this strategy, you will work to find great deals in real estate, write out a contract to get the deal, and then you sell this contract to someone else who is interested. In most cases, the wholesaler is not going to own the property that they are selling. They are instead going to do the work of finding the good properties and then sell this contract over to someone else, attaching a fee to it that will be their profit. Depending on the size of the deal, these fees can be somewhere between $500 and $5000 of profit to the wholesaler.

In some cases, the wholesaler is going to sell off these contracts to various retail buyers, but most of them are going to sell off these contractors to house flippers and other investors who are considered cash buyers. When dealing with a cash buyer, the wholesaler doesn't have to wait for the bank to close the deal so they can get their money within a few days or weeks before moving on.

There are many investors who like to go with this option because it has a high reputation as being easier than one of the other strategies and there aren't really as many start-up costs. You never actually need to own the property so you don't need to worry about banks, tenants, contractors, loan fees, and the costs to fix up the building. It may not make as much potential profit as some of the other strategies, but it is a good one to try out if you don't want to take on the risk of owning your own property.

While there are some great sounding benefits to wholesaling, there is also some work and some risk that is involved. The wholesaler is always on the lookout to find some of the best deals so that they have enough inventory to sell to the other investors. They need to design a good marketing funnel so that they can attract some of the leads as well. You also need to find buyers who are interested in the deals that you find or you will just end up with a lot of properties that you have to pay for and no money to use with them.

Wholesaling is often touted as a method of investing in real estate that doesn't need any money. While you are able to work on the contracts and sell them without having to use any money, you do need to have a few financial resources in order to create the marketing funnel to reach both the sellers and the buyers. But if you are successful at finding the right marketing tunnel for your needs and you can provide some good deals to investors, you can make a great income from this option without spending a lot of money on startup costs.

Chapter 4
Financing Options

Real estate is an expensive investing option you can get into. Many people decide to not get into the investment because they don't have the money sitting around in their savings to help pay for the home and looking for other forms of financing can be expensive and take some time. Coming up with $50,000 or more for a home plus all the money to fix up the home, even if it is a good deal, is hard, and if you don't have any money, or at least not much, you may wonder if it is even possible to get started.

Luckily, there are several financing options that you can choose from. These will help you to get some of the funding that you need to make the purchase and get some of the home improvements done, but you need to be prepared. Banks, portfolio lenders, and other options will want to see that you are prepared and serious about the work that you are undertaking. This means having your finances in order, getting your credit score in line, and having a marketing plan will make it easier to find someone who will provide you with the funds that are necessary to start this investment.

The good news is that over time, it is going to become easier to fund your investment. The banks and other lenders will see that you have experience and success with real estate investing and will be easier on lending you money. You can even save back some of your earnings from your first few sales so that you can do your own funding and don't have to rely on other lenders any longer.

But as a beginner with little capital, you need to find a lender who will take a chance on you and provide you with the funds that you need at competitive rates. Some of the options that you should consider include:

Conventional mortgage

A conventional mortgage is one of the options that you can choose when it comes to purchasing your new property. With a conventional mortgage, you would place a certain percentage down (a conventional one would require twenty percent or more down, but there are other options that ask for less of a down payment if you aren't able to come up with the full amount). These conventional mortgages are going to provide the lowest interest rates, which vary depending on your area, and have the best rates.

With a conventional mortgage, you will need to put in the legwork. Often they will require information about your income history going so many years back, your assets, a good credit score and proof that you will be able to handle your current debts along with the added bill of a new property. Many banks will request additional information such as the marketing plan and you will need to fill out their application before they will even consider you.

To get the best chance of getting a mortgage, you should consider going with a local bank in your area and picking the one that you regularly do business with will help to increase your chances because they already know a lot about you. While the process of getting funding from a bank can take some extra time and is not a fast method to get the money, it is going to offer you the best rates and can save money while owning the home.

203K Loans

This is a sub-set of the FHA loan and it is one that allows an investor to make a purchase on a house that will need some work and it also gives you some ability to finance these repairs. The money for both the cost of the house as well as the repairs are going to be wrapped up into just one loan so you only need to worry about one payment while you own the home and you can use the profits you make from the sale of the home to pay for this. This one will have a low down payment of just 3.5%.

Hard money

This is a financing option that is going to come from individuals or private businesses that know that your intention is to invest in real estate for them. There are different terms that you can place with this kind of funding depending on the agreement that you come up with, but some of the characteristics that are found with this form of funding include:

The loan is going to be based on how much the property is worth.

These are usually short-term loans between 6 months to 3 years.

The interest rate is going to be high for these kinds of loans.

There is a high loan point, which means you are going to have to pay lots of fees on the loan.

Most of the lenders for this are not going to require you to verify your income.

Many of these lenders won't look at your credit report and this transaction is not going to show up on the credit report.

These loans are often funded in just a few days so you can move quickly.

Most of the time the lenders understand that you will need to do some rehab on the property.

If you plan on flipping a home and want to get the money quickly, a hard money loan can be the best ones for you. But you have to move quickly because you are in a hard place if the loan term runs out and you still haven't made a profit on your investment.

Private money

Private money is slightly different than hard money lending because most of the time, hard lenders are professionals and expect the terms to be followed directly (and sometimes the terms are tough), compared to the private money lender who is an individual who wants to make their own investment as well. Sometimes the private money lender will have a close relationship with the investor and they want to help out while making a profit. You will be able to work with the private lender to set up the terms of the money, including the interest that you will pay as well as the length of time it will take to pay the loan back. The private lender also won't receive any equity stake in the property outside their initial investment and the interest rate that you both decided on.

Partnerships

Sometimes getting money for this project on your own can be difficult. Depending on your current income level, debt level, and the amount of money that you want to take out, traditional forms of lending may not work for you. But when you join with someone else and make a partnership, it is easier to get some of the funding that you want.

Banks are going to look more favorably at your funding request when you are in a partnership because they are able to hold two people responsible for paying the money back. They can take both of the incomes as well, which makes the debt to income ratio easier to deal with. Plus, once you own the home, you can both share the work together rather than trying to get it all done on your own. You will have to share the profits, but when you are expanding your portfolio and trying to get your foot in the door with this investment, a partnership may be the answer that you need.

While the ideal situation is to use all of your own money to make the purchases because this can be the easiest, it costs the least amount because you won't have to pay interest or other fees, and you can keep all of the profit. But purchasing a home can be expensive and many real estate investors don't have that kind of money set aside to get started. Using one of these other forms of investing can make it easier to get the money that you need so you can purchase your home, rent it out or flip it, and start making money in real estate.

Chapter 5

Steps to Purchasing the First Property

Now that you have looked around and found the property you want to work with and you have some financing in place, it is time to make a purchase on the property. You need to go through this process the proper way to ensure that you get the property for the price that you want, or close to it, and so you can start on either renting out the property or getting it ready to flip so you don't waste money.

When you are ready to start purchasing your first investment property, follow these simple steps:

1. Decide on the strategy that you want to use. This helps you to determine which properties you want to purchase and makes it easier to keep on track with your end goals.

2. Define your selection criteria. What are you looking for in a property? Is there a certain location that you want to stick with or a good price or do you have some room to wiggle? Do you want a property for a business or for a family to rent out? How much work are you willing to put into this property. Having these outlined ahead of time makes it easier to not get sidetracked by a property that isn't going to meet your needs.

3. Decide what financing you want to use. Since we aren't dealing with a big amount of savings when starting, you will need to

rely on a bank loan or other funding source similar to this, and you must get pre-approved.

4. Look through the MLS or other sites as well as yard signs, direct mail, and the classifieds to see which properties are available. If you are working with the MLS, you may want to bring in a realtor to help you get started. There are a number of good properties that are for sale by owner that you can consider too as these are often lower in price and can be great finds.

5. For each property that you find, go through and see them. Sometimes properties are completely different on paper than they are in person so this is a safe way to make sure that it meets your needs. With each property, make sure to run it through the criteria that you already set so that you can eliminate some that won't work. You may allow for some wiggle room on properties that are good deals but miss out on some of the criteria, but try to stick with these as much as possible to avoid getting stuck with a dud.

6. Make an offer on the property that you want to work with. There are several strategies that come with making and offer and sometimes it depends on how much the seller is asking and how much you are willing to spend, as well as how much of a difference there is between these two numbers. Having some room to negotiate is usually best if possible so offering below your highest amount you are willing to pay, but if this is an issue, go all in the first time and offer your highest bid.

To make the offer, you will need a purchase agreement. Your real estate agent can help you to get this filled out or you can use a fill-in purchase agreement if you aren't working with an agent and plan to purchase a home that is not on the MLS.

7. Negotiate a bit with the seller. It is unlikely that the seller is going to take your original offer so there may be a bit of negotiation that goes on between the two of you. You both may go back and forth a few times until both parties are happy with the terms and the price.

8. This is not the time to skimp out on your work. Take the time to perform all inspections that you can before signing on the purchase. While you are going to be given a list of property details, these inspections help to check out for various issues that could be wrong with the house, makes sure that you are paying a good price, and helps you to know if all the information listed is correct. If something major is wrong with the house that will end up lowering its value or costing you a lot more work, this is still the time that you can get out of the agreement, or even negotiate a lower price with the seller based on the finding. If you forego the inspections, if problems show up later on, you are going to be stuck with them.

9. During this time, you also need to start lining up the work with the contractors. You want to get them into the house as soon as possible after the keys are handed over so that you can get the work done and either start renting it out or get it

resold as quickly as possible. It takes a few months usually to get through all the inspections and the closing of a home, so you will have some time to talk to contractors, get prices figured out, and set up dates when everyone should be there.

10. Once the inspections are all done and you are happy with the results, it is time to visit a Title and Escrow office (or an attorney's office) to sign all the papers. Then the paperwork is recorded and you own the home now. You can get the home ready and then start listing out for new tenants or working to make changes so that the home can be flipped and resold as quickly as possible.

The process is going to work pretty similarly to this when talking about residential or commercial real estate as well. You must always make sure that you are getting a good deal on the property that you pick and it is important to do inspections to make sure that nothing is hidden in the property that could make you lose money. But if you follow your criteria and work with the right people who can take care of all the legal stuff, you will soon own a real estate investment and can decide what you would like to do with it to turn it into a money maker.

Chapter 6

Working with Brokers and Property Managers

When you are getting started with real estate, there are many people you will have to work with to get the property purchased, fixed up, and rented out or sold. While it would be nice to do all the work on our own, there are other people who come into the mix to help with the various parts that the investor will encounter during this process. Learning how to work with real estate brokers and your property managers (if you are renting out the property) can make a world of difference on the amount of profit that you can make in this investment. Let's take a look at how each of them works to help you get the best return on investment with this opportunity.

Working with your broker

When it comes to buying and selling a property, most investors choose to work with a real estate broker. This allows them a lot of benefits whether they are purchasing or selling their property, and can really save a lot of money and time in the long run.

First, when it comes to purchasing a property, your real estate broker should be the first person you call to find a place. These individuals know the area you are in and can give insights as to where the prices are now and where they may go in the near future. They have connections all over town and may hear about a great deal on a property long before you would find out about it yourself. They are a great resource to ask questions of and to work with to find the perfect property to start out with.

Once you find your property, your real estate broker will be able to pull up all the paperwork to help you put in an offer and to do negotiations until both you and the seller are happy with the price. The broker can walk you through all the paperwork that needs to be done with the inspections and goes with you all the way through closing until the keys are in your hand.

After you have some time to fix up the house or rent it out and you are ready to sell it again, you may find that working with a realtor can make a difference. Some investors like to try to sell the home on their own, but a broker has a lot of resources and connections and often it will save you time (and money in the long run) to work right with them. They can again walk you through the whole process until you get to closing, which can be helpful for someone who is just starting out with this option.

It is important that you find a good broker you get along with. If you plan on staying in real estate for a long time, there is the potential of many different purchase and sales, and it is nice to work with the same individual through them all. You can both get used to each other's styles and you can ask questions, find out deals, and really see your income grow when you find the right broker to work with.

Working with a good property manager

Depending on how much time you plan to spend on your rental properties, you may find that hiring a property manager is a good choice for you. As your portfolio grows, these property managers can make things easier on you, especially if you are still working your regular job. They can help to pick out good tenants to rent the building, perform any of the maintenance that is needed in the property, receive rental payments, and more. While you can do this on your own if you just have a few properties, a property manager has the experience factor and can take some of the stress from you.

When you are looking for a good property manager, you should look for a couple key things such as:

- How many properties they manage: you want to make sure that the property manager is giving your property the time and attention that it deserves. If the property manager already has too many projects going on, you may want to choose someone who can devote more attention to your project.

- How much they charge: most property managers will charge between seven and ten percent of the rental income revenue, so ask your options how much they will charge. If they are trying to get a number that is way above this, be careful with hiring them.

- What software they use: there are various forms of software your property manager can use to record costs and rental income so ask them about what they use and why they chose that one.

- Do they do routine inspections: some property managers balk at the idea of doing a routine property inspection or they will try to add on extra fees in order to do this. But how is the property manager doing their job if they never inspect the property? Yes, they do need to be respectful of the tenant and allow plenty of notice so the tenant knows they are going to be there, but if a property manager is making it difficult to do routine inspections on the property, you need to find another option.

- Do you get along with them: there are some property managers who assume they know best, try to finish your sentences, or are always interrupting you. If you see this in one of the property managers you are talking to, it may be best to go with someone else. You won't want to deal with this kind of behavior when something is going on in one of your properties.

Picking a property manager is a great way to make sure that your properties are under good care when you aren't able to be around all the time, but you still want to make sure that you pick a good manager to take over. Check out a few different options and talk to each of them personally so you can understand their system and how they will take care of you, your tenants, and your property.

Chapter 7

Asset Protection—Consider LLC and Other Options to Keep Your Assets Safe

What some beginners in real estate don't understand is that this investment is a business type. They decide to get into the investment and get some funding, but they never treat it like a business or worry about protecting their assets. But if you don't set this investment up like an asset, you are going to run into trouble. When someone gets hurt on the property or something else goes wrong, you will be the one held liable and without the right business setup, your personal assets can be taken down as well. Here we are going to talk about some of the most common business types and which one you should pick to help you make money in real estate without risking your assets.

Sole Proprietor

If you don't pick a business entity, you are going to be considered a sole proprietor. This is an individual who runs their business and is responsible for everything that goes on in the business. You will trade under your own name and there is no separation of liabilities and assets. This can be nice because it makes things simple and you won't have to spend much time filing paperwork, but if someone comes after your business, they can come after your personal assets as well.

Limited Liability Company

This one is kind of a hybrid between a corporation and a partnership. Members in this kind of business organization are going to have some of the income benefits and flexibility that come from being a sole proprietor or a partnership (with less paperwork to deal with as well, while still getting some of the limited liability if something goes wrong. There are some legal differences that you will have to keep up with and you will need to follow the legal requirements to become one of these, but there is considerable more freedom with this option while still getting a lot of the protection that you need.

Corporation

It is unlikely that you will want to become a corporation when working in real estate in the beginning because this is going to include a legal entity that is large and will need to file a lot of extra paperwork in order to be legal. You will need to file articles of incorporation in your state and you will often work with stockholders, which can limit some of the freedom of decision that you would like. The nice thing about this though is that you can get some tax-free benefits, like health insurance and other tax deductions on your business while using this one. If you are working with a C-corporation, you will need to be careful about the possibility of double taxation that occurs with the profits as well as taxes that happen on stockholder dividends.

S-corporation

This one is also known as a small business corporation and these are corporations that are designed to get a tax advantage, as long as requirements are met with the IRS. The corporate taxes are going to be waved and the owners of the company would just report their income on their personal tax returns so they won't have to worry about the double taxation that can happen.

For the most part, you will not want to work with a corporation because this is for bigger entities and the double taxation is going to cost you a lot of money, but while the sole proprietor may seem tempting, you won't want to go with this option either because it limits the amount of protection that you are going to get.

For real estate investing, most investors choose to go with the LLC option. This gives them the next mix between the sole proprietorship and the corporation. You will be able to be in control of this form of business entity and you won't have to listen to the views of stockholders to get things done, but you still get the protection of your personal assets with the structure. If you do decide to become a corporation, most of the time it is best to register as the s-corporation because it will save you money from the double taxation that occurs with normal corporations.

As a beginner, you may assume that it doesn't matter if you set yourself up as a business entity at all but there are a lot of things that could happen with one of your properties. What if you hire a contractor who falls or gets hurt on the property or something happens with one of your tenants while they are living in the building? Without the right business entity in place, the individual in question could come after not only your business assets but also your personal assets. But with the help of a good business entity in place, you can protect yourself and deal more with the tasks of running your investment.

Chapter 8
Options on Lease Types to Protect Your Investment

Picking out the right type of lease for your properties can help to ensure that you get the income that you want out of your hard work. These leases are going to help protect both you and the tenant when followed correctly, but you do need to lay out the terms of the agreement early on to help avoid issues with that pays what and how the property should be treated. Some of the lease types that you can choose for your real estate properties include:

Residential property leases

Residential leases are a bit different than what you would find with commercial properties and sometimes it is going to vary based on the property that you have. For example, if you are dealing with a single family home, you may want to consider having the tenant pay their own utilities, while most apartment buildings will lump this in with the rent to keep things easier. Here we will discuss a few of the options for residential property leases:

Short term: most residential property leases are going to be at least a year long, but in some cases, you may want to offer them for a shorter amount of time, such as six months. Sometimes families are moving to an area or need a place for just a few months before moving on, and you can offer this service to them. The monthly rates on these are going to be higher, but they are also harder to fill in most cases.

Long term: most properties like to stick with one year, but as an incentive, you may choose to offer a discount to those who agree to stick around for two years or more. This provides you with a steadier income and keeps the tenant around. Sometimes between one and two years is the average and then when the lease is done, both parties can renegotiate the lease.

When picking out the lease that you want to choose, consider what all will be covered. In single family homes, most landlords will have the tenants pay for their own utilities and water while the landlord is going to be responsible for the taxes and any maintenance. In bigger complexes, it is easier to group the utilities together and add that to the rental payments each month. Decide what other extras you would like to include in this to save some time and to ensure that both parties are on the same page.

Also, make sure to list out the responsibilities of the tenant. For example, they are responsible for paying their rent on time (or you can begin the eviction process) and they are responsible for taking care of the property and not allowing more than normal wear and tear damage to happen inside the property.

Commercial property leases

There are many options available when it comes to leasing in commercial properties and sometimes it depends on your area and the tenants that you get into the building and the amount that you think that you will make. Some of the options for leases with commercial properties include:

Full service or gross lease

With this kind of lease, the rent is going to include everything. The landlord is going to pay for everything on the property including the janitorial services, utilities, taxes, insurance, and even maintenance. The landlord will have to figure out how much this will be and then charges the tenants their share to get this covered. In some cases, in order to protect the landlord, the tenant may be charged extra on the rent if they use what is considered excess utility consumption. This is easy for the tenant because they have just one bill to take care of everything so they are willing to pay a bit higher in rent for this option.

Net lease

Another option is known as the net lease. This one is going to end up with a lower amount of rent to the tenant which will include the rent to use the space as well as what is known as the usual costs, which would include things like maintenance, and which the landlord is going to pay. There are several options that fall into this category including:

- Single net lease: with this lease, the tenant is able to pay a lower base rent, but they will also do a pro-rated share of the property tax, which is something that all tenants will have to pay a share of based on how much room they take up in the building. The landlord is going to pay some of the other expenses of the building by the tenant would pay their own janitorial services and utilities.

- Double net lease: this is where the tenant is going to be responsible for the base rent as well as their part of the insurance and property tax. The landlord will take care of the maintenance of the building, but the tenant is still in charge of their utilities.

- Triple net lease: this one can be really popular in commercial real estate. With this one, the tenant is going to pay for the base monthly rent as well as the utilities, common area utilities, insurance, and property taxes. The tenant would also pay for their own utilities and janitorial services along with taxes and insurance. This one is often going to favor the landlord because the tenant is going to pay for everything, but there are some benefits to the tenant as well, including transparency to their customers.

There are many options that come with picking out a lease with commercial properties and working out the best option that will attract the right companies into the area while still making a good profit. Carefully consider each of these options before deciding to ensure you get the best option for both you and your tenant.

Chapter 9

Costly Mistakes to Avoid as a Beginner

It is all too common for beginners to get into the market, excited to give it a try and make some money, but they are just not prepared. They don't think their decisions all the way through and are ready to just get started. This rushing can cause them to make some mistakes in the real estate market that can prove pretty costly and can end your investment in no time. As a beginner, here are some of the costly mistakes that you should avoid if you want to really see your investment work for you.

Not having a marketing plan

Real estate investing is just like a business and you need to treat it as such if you want to see success. A marketing plan can help to bring the different parts of the business together and it can really help you to define your goals and your timeline for achieving some of these goals. First, when you approach the bank to get some of the funding that you need, you will be required to not only have information on your income and credit history, but they will want to see your marketing or business plan to determine you are ready.

While a marketing plan may seem like it takes up a lot of time and isn't really necessarily, if you want to see success, you need to have this business plan in place. Consistently, beginners and professionals who have this marketing plan (and who have it all written out) are more likely to find success compared to those who never make one of these plans.

Starting a business or marketing plan can be tough and you may not know where to start. There are several business plans available online that you can use for your needs. Just go online and find the one that you like the best and then fill in the blanks to make it relevant for your real estate business.

Not learning about the available resources

Getting started in real estate is tough enough, why not use some of the resources that are available for you. There are professional organizations full of professionals and beginners you can join to ask questions and use some of the resources that they have in their area to make your business more successful. You can talk to your brokerage, your colleagues, read magazines, talk to realtors and find all the resources in your area.

Some beginners are so sure that they know the best steps to take to see success that they push aside others who may be able to get advice and after they get started, they refuse to read up on new changes in the market and miss out on changes in the marketing cycle, and they just end up costing themselves a lot of money. It doesn't take that much time to use the resources in your area and they can really help you to get more out of your investment.

Getting into a bidding war

When it is possible, you should never get into a bidding war with others over a property. While there may be a great property that you want, once you get into a bidding war with someone else, you are risking letting the emotions get in the way. You become more invested in the property and you may get into the mindset that you don't want to let this property go and your whole marketing plan and selection criteria go out the door and you start going on your emotions.

If you get into a bidding war and find that others are going for the same property, it is probably best to just let the property go. Otherwise, if the emotions start going and you get stuck in a loop of not wanting to let it go, you are going to end up paying a lot more for the property than you can afford or even what the property is worth. Remember that bidding wars are great for the seller because it increases the amount that you will be able to earn on the home, but it can be a pain for investors who want to get the house for a low price.

The same idea comes into play when working on auctions. You can find some great deals on homes at various auctions. Some of the homes need a lot of work while others are just properties the owner wants to get rid of quickly. Depending on the amount of interest in the home, the price can either stay at an affordable rate and you can get it for below the market value, or the price can go way up as more and more people bid for the property. If you do decide to go to an auction to get some deals, pick out the maximum that you are willing to spend on the property and don't go higher than that no matter what.

Not learning the language

As you look through all the classifieds and advertisements that come with the real estate world, you need to learn some of the language that is used on that end. Realtors and homeowners want to make their home appear as a great deal, no matter what kind it is, and they will use different words to help make this happen. Understanding the language that is in the listings you see can make it easier to determine if a home is going to meet some of your criteria before you even go and visit it.

For example, a listing that uses the word "cozy" means that the home is going to be small. A listing that states the home "as is" means that there is going to be a lot of work to fix up the property. If you see that there are quite a few exclamation marks in place, this means that there is not much information about the place. Always remember that if a property sounds too good, it probably is one that you should avoid, or at least go and visit before making any decisions.

Making a purchase without seeing the home

With how busy our world is, it can be tempting to try and get a property without having to do as much of the work. But you should never purchase a property based on some of the pictures you see online. Always go to the property and actually see what is going on with it. Walk in all the rooms and check out all the corners. Without this, it is likely that you are getting into a bad deal that is going to cost you a lot of money.

Pictures and virtual tours never work out well if you don't see the property. They are great for the seller to get a good idea of the layout of the building and to make some decisions about if this property is even something they are interested in, but the house is going to look much different than the pictures that the seller presents. Of course, the seller is going to post pictures that show the home in the best light possible. But when you get to the home, you may notice that the rooms appear smaller, the garage is in a weird location on the property, the neighbor has some loud dogs that bark all day long, or other issues that will affect how well you will be able to sell the property or rent it out later on. Always go and see the property in person before you get too attached or decide to purchase the home.

Underestimating your budget

It is important to come up with a budget that is realistic to helping you get the home purchased and fixed up before renting out or selling. Many times as a beginner it is easier to assume that the prices will be lower, but then you have to come up with money that you don't have later in order to get the property fixed up for your customers.

First, make sure that you set a realistic budget when it comes to picking out a home. While you own this home, you will not only have to pay off your current bills and obligations, but you will also need to handle the payments for mortgage, insurance, taxes, and any costs for contractors and remodeling for the new property. Before you go out looking in the market, you need to look at your budget and determine exactly how much you are able to afford for all these payments combined inside of your current budget.

Understanding how much you are able to afford in remodels is important as well. Talking to contractors and other workers to get a good idea of expenses is important to getting numbers down, but you should add a little bit to these costs in case unexpected things come up. It is always better to have a budget that is too high rather than running out of money and being stuck with a home you can't do anything with for a long time.

Bathroom and kitchen remodels

Whether you plan to use this home as a rental property or you are going to sell the property, it is usually not worth your time to remodel the kitchen or the bathroom. These areas can look a lot better when you do some work to them and make some updates, but they cost a lot of money. Doing a whole kitchen and bathroom remodel is a big waste of money when you want to flip a home and you will not get your money back for the short time you own the property.

This doesn't mean that you can't make some improvements to these areas to help them to look better. Some of the homes that you purchase are going to need some serious work and one of the areas you can improve include the bathroom and kitchen. But finding some inexpensive hacks to clean these areas up instead of doing a whole remodel will help the areas to look better without having to waste money on a complete remodel.

Not being active in the process

No matter what part you plan to play in this investment or if you plan to hand this over to a property manager later on, you still need to be an involved participant. From looking for the homes that you want to purchase to making the purchase agreement to all the inspections that need to happen and the closing, you need to be involved and you need to know what is going on in the property. When it comes to making some of the remodels and fixes to the home, even if you hire a contractor you must still be around to make sure the work is progressing. Being around when tenants are being chosen or during the selling process are important as well.

This is your investment, and if you want it to be successful, you need to make sure that you are involved. There are a lot of different parts that go into real estate investing and if you aren't around, you can quickly get lost and little details, that could end up costing you a lot of money, can easily be ignored or handled the wrong way. Don't trust your investment to others who may not have your best interests at heart; make sure that you are always involved in all aspects of your investment.

As a beginner, it is easy to fall behind on some parts of the process because you just don't know what is going on or what you should be doing. But some of the mistakes that many beginners make can end up costing you a lot of money and can make your business unsuccessful. Make sure to avoid some of the mistakes that we discussed in this guidebook, and you can help to protect your investment and avoid losing unnecessary money.

Conclusion

Thank for making it through to the end of *Real Estate Investing: How to Invest in Real Estate with Little Money and No Experience*. Let's hope it was informative and able to provide you with all of the tools you need to achieve your goals of

The next step is to get out there and make your first investment into real estate. This guidebook provided you with some of the most important steps that you can take to go from beginner to expert in the real estate market. Inside, we spent time learning about the different options to choose for investing, how to pick out your investing strategy, how to make your purchase, and how to avoid some common mistakes.

There are many different aspects that come with investing in real estate and it may feel challenging to figure out where to get started. This guidebook will answer your questions and help give you the tools that you need to get started with this investment today!

Finally, if you found this book useful in any way, a review on Amazon is always appreciated!